99 Postcards
for Georges Perec
Matt Fallaize

KFS
PAMPHLETS

Newton-le-Willows

Published in the United Kingdom in 2019
by The Knives Forks And Spoons Press,
51 Pipit Avenue,
Newton-le-Willows,
Merseyside,
WA12 9RG.

ISBN 978-1-912211-36-4

Supported using public funding by
ARTS COUNCIL
ENGLAND
LOTTERY FUNDED

*"For Rowena Fallaize, there's no one I'd
rather be half-way up the M6 with"*

1.

The flat plains of Lancashire
I've bought a new book, weather
Bracing, having a time x

2.

Here we are in Jersey, weather good
Learning Spanish from the waiter
Fond regards

3.

On a cliff!
In Cornwall!
Such Views! (out of breath)

4.

Hi from a disused
Railway platform in Corfe Castle
The butterflies love the silence

5.

Greetings from Southport
I'm out of money for slots.
Ask dad for me, hugs

6.

Halfway up the M6
I've bought a card reading
Greetings from halfway up the M6

7.

In Dorset the light
On a pool has convinced
Me I'm three again

8.

In Damascus
Out of my depth
Cancel the milk

9.

Norway cruise, so serene, the
Ghosts of possibility melt
Into the ice-wall, say hi to Mum

10.

There are others at a dam we used
To go to, the family's scattered now
Got friends to send a card

11.

Just up the road!
Can see our house!
Should probably go home

12.

On a bank next to the sea
Saying goodbye to Nick
The Atlantic's still, today

13.

We're in Northern Italy!
We're supposed to be in Southern Italy.
We're not speaking, kisses.

14.

Sunburnt in Egypt, waiters
So friendly but feel they're
Holding something back

15.

In Finisterre, it lives up
To the name, my world is ending
Back the 14th

16.

Living it up in Vegas, baby!
Food terrible, may be developing
Gambling addiction, love to all

17.

Hello from the Lake District!
Weather poor, people very white
Got cramp, back next week

18.

In Stoke
Not sure how
Will write soon

19.

Hola from Barcelona! Food
Excellent, having crisis
Of confidence, kisses

20.

Quick note from Joburg
Am implicated in murder
Regards to the Mrs

21.

In Trieste, not how
I imagined though I
Don't know what I imagined

22.

Watching the same views
As you once did. It's still.
Back in a week

23.

In Fuerteventura
It's harder than you'd imagine
To buy a pen, please feed the cat

24.

Experiencing Damascene conversion
Not even in Syria, now
Funny how it turns out, hugs

25.

The stillness of a
Summer night in Bergen
Love to the kids

26.

In Ireland for the most part
Teetering on the divide
Geographically, of course

27.

Konichiwa from Tokyo
Not really sure what to say
Slightly overwhelmed

28.

Greetings from Hoy
On fire
Waiting for poets

29.

In N'Awlins the
Chocolate in my pocket
Has melted, say hi to Nan

30.

Can't move in Cancun
Been invited to a party
Not going, back soon

31.

Remind me not
To holiday in Edinburgh
In August, no seriously, kisses

32.

Here on the Cornish Riviera!
Such nice people, played
Card games, love to all

33.

In Longsight and
I think I'm being followed
Wish you were here

34.

The silence of Finnish
Sun thinking about composing
Quartets, miss you

35.

The Sahara, utter darkness
People lovely have been sold
Many souvenirs, back 12th

36.

Somewhere on a canal,
Surprisingly entertained looking
For postbox

37.

Halfway down the side
Of the Cat and Fiddle hard
To write upside down, best wishes

38.

At a wedding I
Really wish I wasn't at
Food ok, speak soon

39.

We're walking the Pennines
I feel under-dressed and drab
Plus ça change, see you next week

40.

On a twelve stretch
In Strangeways
You were right about Dave, love

41.

On Billy's stag! Not overly
Happy about the prostitutes
Don't tell Mum

42.

A sharp jag of light
Flat and hard off
Coniston Water, love to all

43.

In Split and red wine is
Layered on orange juice and my
Parents are smiling should write

44.

Up a mountain and
Rethinking things may
Take a while, back soon?

45.

In Ormskirk forgot
To go on holiday
Not sure why writing

46.

In the Ozarks and am
Growing bored of banjos
Who'd have thought? Hugs

47.

Solo in London its
Not as fun as I thought
Miss you, miss the boys

48.

The great wall of China!
Quite long. Quite tired
Back Thursday week

49.

In Stockholm, coming
Down with something
Say hi to Raymond

50.

The equator, nothing
Equivocal it's hot
Night drops. Love

51.

Greetings from Tallinn
This is a postcard out
Of ideas. Back soon.

52.

Watching Sequoias
Grow in the Sierra Nevada
May be some time

53.

Hello from Cambridge I'm
Disconnected from events
Can't imagine myself, write soon

54.

On a hog on route 66
No crisis here! It's
Dusty, back in a month

55.

In the Niger delta and
Being very precise. There
Are ospreys, back summer

56.

Impossible refraction the
Light from the Eiger viewed
and reviewed, back Wednesday

57.

At home wondering why
I'm sending the postcard
When it's you on holiday

58.

Narcoleptic in Dhaka
Bullied by heat and
Memory love to all

59.

Chased by ghosts in
Paris, I blame John Cale
Back at some point

60.

Adrift on a boating
Lake in Blackpool I can see
Your house from here

61.

Hello from Sochi! (this
part excised) too long!
See you at the finish!

62.

In Azincourt of saintly G.P
Amazing, holding it all in
Back soon x x

63.

In Mumbai mistaken
For Australian all rounder
Now rich, bonzer

64.

Phoning Tom Waits from
Istanbul have yet
To hear back, hugs

65.

Back to Boscastle it's
As it always was, missed
It, miss you

66.

Hello from Abersoch I can't
Possibly afford the houses
Best come home

67.

Blending in with the fossils
On the Jurassic Coast
Love to all (trilobites)

68.

In Milan like St Sebastian
Not feeling lucky, did you
Water the plants? X

__ hold on

69.

Midway between Qatar and Switzerland
With a briefcase full of money
Everyone seems so nice!

70.

At Old Bailey, not allowed
To write this postcard can't
Say when back, kisses?

71.

Evading the truth on the A39
Writing from a cafe, poor
Food, in a rush, back soon

72.

Le Grand Départ! Yorkshire
Yorkshire what's the French
For by eckerslike?

73.

Quick note from Gaza
This is murder
Please stop. Love.

74.

Invigorated in Nanjing you
Can hear the economy growing!
Back next week, kisses

75.

Writing this from the departure
Lounge, working up the
Nerve. Love to all

76.

This card written
From the past she's
On a forgotten beach

77.

Feeling the earth
Move in Banks, don't
Like the implication. Kisses

78.

In Guadalajara fomenting
Revolution, reading Yeats
And Duhig, love to the Mrs

79.

Listening vainly for the
Sound of bees in our garden
Not far to the postbox

80.

Sharp Flanders horizon my
Imagination is failing me
Back Wednesday x

81.

Climbing the hills outside Oldham
Looking for something, unsure what
Give everyone my love x

82.

In Lynmouth and it's
Starting to rain, be back
As soon as possible x

83.

Two weeks in Scotland
I may be a foreigner
By the end, love to all

84.

Painting watercolours
By the sea in Dieppe
Back in a year, much love

85.

On Ilkley Moor, remembered
To bring my hat. Just as well
Get the heating on

86.

Darkest Herefordshire and
Looking for badgers not
Sure how many, love to Dad

87.

Eating fried dough sticks and
Fielding pitying glances in Beijing
Back next week, kisses

88.

Still in Stoke
This is ridiculous
Will try again

89.

Tag from Munchen! If
There's enough cultural relevance
Turn out you can drink as much as you like

90.

En route to the fens I decided
To walk, am undecided about
This, back in a fortnight

91.

Setting sail for Brussels in
Search of a static image
Back when it's all over

92.

Night falling on Hoboken
For seventeen peaceful minutes
Diffuse light and tangible calm

93.

Adrift in Kendal. It's still
Raining, it's always raining
The postman just floated by

94.

In holding pattern over
Gatwick In holding pattern
Over Gatwick in holding

95.

Hello from Geneva for
Obvious reasons I shan't
Write further. I love you all.

96.

Still coming back to Boscastle
Never really left
My image is in the rock, back Tuesday

97.

At home with my
Newborn son and wouldn't wish
To be anywhere else

98.

This postcard sent
More in hope than
Expectation.

99.

Closing a notebook back
Where I started, closing the door
And walking away. Hello.

Lightning Source UK Ltd.
Milton Keynes UK
UKHW021223040919

349161UK00001B/24/P